POEMS

POEMS
1950-1965

ROBERT CREELEY

MARION BOYARS
LONDON

First Published in Great Britain 1966
by Calder and Boyars Ltd

Reprinted by Marion Boyars Publishers Ltd 1978
18 Brewer Street, London, W.1

Copyright © 1962, 1966, 1978 Robert Creeley

ISBN 0 7145 0475 0 Hardcover
ISBN 0 7145 0476 9 Paperback

Printed in Great Britain by
Biddles Ltd, Guildford, Surrey

for Bobbie—
who makes all things possible

Poems in Parts 1 and 2 were first collected as follows:

All in Part 1, except "Naughty Boy," in THE WHIP by Robert Creeley (Migrant Books, 1957)

"Naughty Boy" and all in Part 2 in A FORM OF WOMEN by Robert Creeley . (Jargon Books in association with Corinth Books, copyright 1959 Robert Creeley)

Some of the poems in Part 2 first appeared in the United States in the following periodicals: *Black Mountain Review, Poetry* (Chicago), *Evergreen Review, Measure, The Naked Ear, Texas Quarterly, Neon* (Supplement to *Now*), *Hearse, Yugen, Ark II Moby I, Inland.*

Some of the poems in Part 3 first appeared in the United States in the following periodicals: *Between Worlds, Big Table, Chelsea, Elizabeth, Folio, Inscape, New Directions Annual, The Nation, National Review, Poetry* (Chicago), *Quagga, Trobar, White Dove Review, Yugen.*

Some of the poems in Part 4 first appeared in the United States and England in the following periodicals: *Agenda, Arbor, Beloit Poetry Journal, Broadside Poems #6, Burning Deck, Chicago Choice, El Corno Emplumado, Encounter, Fubbalo, Fuck You, Granta, King Ida's Watch Chain, The Lugano Review, My Own Mag, The Nation, Niagara Frontier Review, Origin, Outcry, Oyez, The Paris Review, Poetry, The Resuscitator, Underdog, The Vassar Review, Wild Dog, Writing, Yale Literary Magazine.*

PREFACE

Wherever it is one stumbles (to get to wherever) at least some way will exist, so to speak, as and when a man takes this or that step—for which, god bless him. Insofar as these poems are such places, always they were ones stumbled into: warmth for a night perhaps, the misdirected intention come right; and too, a sudden instance of love, and the being loved, wherewith a man also contrives a world (of his own mind).

It seems to me, now, that I know less of these poems than will a reader, at least the reader for whom—if I write for anyone—I have written. How much I should like to please! It is a constant concern.

That is, however, hopeful and pompous, and not altogether true. I write poems because it pleases me, very much—I think that is true. In any case, we live as we can, each day another—there is no use in counting. Nor more, say, to live than what there is, to live. I want the poem as close to this fact as I can bring it; or it, me.

R. C.

CONTENTS

3 1959-1960

4 1961-1965

1 1950 - 1955

HART CRANE

for Slater Brown

I

He had been stuttering, by the edge
of the street, one foot still
on the sidewalk, and the other
in the gutter . . .

like a bird, say, wired to flight, the
wings, pinned to their motion, stuffed.

The words, several, and for each, several
senses.
          "It is very difficult to sum up
briefly . . ."
                    It always was.

(Slater, let me come home.
The letters have proved insufficient.
The mind cannot hang to them as it could
to the words.

There are ways beyond
what I have here to work with,
what my head cannot push to any kind
of conclusion.

But my own ineptness
cannot bring them to hand,
the particulars of those times
we had talked.)

"Men kill themselves because they are
afraid of death, he says . . ."

The push
          beyond and
into

2

Respect, they said he respected the
ones with the learning, lacking it
himself

     (Waldo Frank & his
6 languages)

        What had seemed
important
While Crane sailed to Mexico I was writing
(so that one betrayed

            himself)
He slowed
     (without those friends to keep going, to
keep up), stopped
         dead and the head could not
go further

     without those friends

. . . *And so it was I entered the broken world*

Hart Crane.

     Hart

LE FOU

for Charles

       who plots, then, the lines
       talking, taking, always the beat from
       the breath
              (moving slowly at first
       the breath
              which is slow—

       I mean, graces come slowly,
       it is that way.

       So slowly (they are waving
       we are moving
              away from   (the trees
                    the usual   (go by
       which is slower than this, is
                   (we are moving!
       goodbye

A SONG

for Ann

I had wanted a quiet testament
and I had wanted, among other things,
a song.
         That was to be
of a like monotony.
                    (A grace

Simply. Very very quiet.
                        A murmur of some lost
thrush, though I have never seen one.

Which was you then. Sitting
and so, at peace, so very much now this same quiet.

A song.

And of you the sign now, surely, of a gross
perpetuity
           (which is not reluctant, or if it is,
it is no longer important.

A song.

Which one sings, if he sings it,
with care.

THE CRISIS

Let me say (in anger) that since the day we were married
we have never had a towel
where anyone could find it,
the fact.
       Notwithstanding that I am not
simple to live with, not
my own judgement, but no
matter.
       There are other things:

to kiss you is not
to love you.
       Or not so simply.

Laughter releases rancor, the quality of mercy is not
strained.

FOR RAINER GERHARDT

Impossible, rightly, to define these
conditions of
friendship, the wandering & inexhaustible wish to
be of use, somehow
to be helpful

when it isn't simple,—wish
otherwise, convulsed, and leading
nowhere I can go.

What one knows, then, not
simple, convulsed, and feeling
(this night)
petulance of all conditions, not
wondered, not even
felt.

I have felt nothing, I have
felt that if it were simpler, and
being so, it were a matter only of
an incredible indifference
(to us)
they might say it all—

but not friends, the
acquaintances, but you,
Rainer. And likely there is
petulance in us
kept apart.

THE RIDDLE

What it is, the literal size
incorporates.
                    The question
is a mute question. One is
too lonely, one wants
to stop there, at the edge of

conception. The woman

imperative, the man
lost in stern
thought:

give it form certainly,
the name and titles.

(Hogpen, deciduous growth, etc.
making neither much dent
nor any feeling: the trees completely
or incompletely
attached to ground

During which time all the time sounds of an anterior conversation
and what are they talking
about

Cares mount. My own
certainly
as much as anyone else's.
                              Between
each and every row of seats
put a table
and put on that
an ashtray

        (Who don't know what I know
in what proportion, is either off, too much
or on.

        Look it up, check
or if that's too much, say, too time-consuming or whatever other
neat adjective to attach to any
distraction
        (for doing nothing at all.

The rites are care, the natures
less simple, the mark of hell knows what but
something, the trace of

line, trace of
line made by someone

Ultimate: no man shall go unattended.
No man shall be an idiot for purely exterior reasons.

THE RHYME

There is the sign of
the flower—
to borrow the theme.

But what or where to recover
what is not love
too simply.

I saw her
and behind her there were
flowers, and behind them
nothing.

THE INNOCENCE

Looking to the sea, it is a line
of unbroken mountains.

It is the sky.
It is the ground. There
we live, on it.

It is a mist
now tangent to another
quiet. Here the leaves
come, there
is the rock in evidence

or evidence.
What I come to do
is partial, partially kept.

THE BALL GAME

The one damn time (7th inning)
standing up to get a hot dog someone spills
mustard all over me.

                The conception is
the hit, whacko!
Likewise out of the park

of our own indifferent vulgarity, not
mind you, that one repents even the most visual
satisfaction.

Early in life the line is straight
made straight
against the grain.

Take the case of myself, and why not
since these particulars need
no further impetus,
                take me at the age of 13
and for some reason there, no matter the particular
reason.

       The one damn time (7th inning)
standing up to get a hot dog someone spills
mustard all over me.

THE CARNIVAL

Whereas the man who hits
the gong dis-
proves it, in all its
simplicity—

         Even so the attempt
makes for triumph, in
another man.

Likewise in love I
am not foolish or in-
competent. My method is not a

tenderness, but hope
defined.

AFTER LORCA

for M. Marti

The church is a business, and the rich
are the business men.
When they pull on the bells, the
poor come piling in and when a poor man dies, he has a wooden
cross, and they rush through the ceremony.

But when a rich man dies, they
drag out the Sacrament
and a golden Cross, and go *doucement, doucement*
to the cemetery.

And the poor love it
and think it's crazy.

THE KIND OF ACT OF

Giving oneself to the dentist or doctor who is a good one,
to take the complete
possession of mind, there is no

giving. The mind
beside the act of any dispossession is

lecherous. There is no more giving in
when there is no more sin.

THE DISHONEST MAILMEN

They are taking all my letters, and they
put them into a fire.

                     I see the flames, etc.
But do not care, etc.

They burn everything I have, or what little
I have. I don't care, etc.

The poem supreme, addressed to
emptiness—this is the courage

necessary. This is something
quite different.

THE CROW

The crow in the cage in the dining-room
hates me, because I will not feed him.

And I have left nothing behind in leaving
because I killed him.

And because I hit him over the head with a stick
there is nothing I laugh at.

Sickness is the hatred of a repentance
knowing there is nothing he wants.

THE IMMORAL PROPOSITION

If you never do anything for anyone else
you are spared the tragedy of human relation-

ships. If quietly and like another time
there is the passage of an unexpected thing:

to look at it is more
than it was. God knows

nothing is competent nothing is
all there is. The unsure

egoist is not
good for himself.

FOR W. C. W.

The pleasure of the wit sustains
a vague aroma

The fox-glove (unseen) the
wild flower

To the hands come
many things. In time of trouble

a wild exultation.

APPLE UPPFLE

Vanity (like a belly
dancer's romance) : just
the hope. The unafraid & naked

wish, helpless. Pushed against a
huge & unending door . . .

And while the mind
a little more tenuous, more careful of it,
crabwise, gives in . . .

To the pleasure of a meal in silence.

THE OPERATION

By Saturday I said you would be better on Sunday.
The insistence was a part of a reconciliation.

Your eyes bulged, the grey
light hung on you, you were hideous.

My involvement is just an old
habitual relationship.

Cruel, cruel to describe
what there is no reason to describe.

CHANSON

Oh, le petit rondelay!
Gently, gently.
It is that I grow older.

As when for a lark
gaily, one hoists up a window
shut many years.

Does the lady's eye grow moist-
er, is it madame's in-
clination,

etc. Oh, le petit rondelay!
Gently, gently.
It is that I grow older.

Riding the horse as was my wont,
there was a bunch of cows in a field.

The horse
chased

them. I likewise, an uneasy
accompanist.

To wit, the Chinese proverb goes:
if you lie in a field

and fall asleep,
you will be found in a field

asleep.

THE CONSPIRACY

You send me your poems,
I'll send you mine.

Things tend to awaken
even through random communication.

Let us suddenly
proclaim spring. And jeer

at the others,
all the others.

I will send a picture too
if you will send me one of you.

I KNOW A MAN

As I sd to my
friend, because I am
always talking,—John, I

sd, which was not his
name, the darkness sur-
rounds us, what

can we do against
it, or else, shall we &
why not, buy a goddamn big car,

drive, he sd, for
christ's sake, look
out where yr going.

THE END

When I know what people think of me
I am plunged into my loneliness. The grey

hat bought earlier sickens.
I have no purpose no longer distinguishable.

A feeling like being choked
enters my throat.

THE DEATH OF VENUS

I dreamt her sensual proportions
had suffered sea-change,

that she was a porpoise, a
sea-beast rising lucid from the mist.

The sound of waves killed speech
but there were gestures—

of my own, it was to call her closer,
of hers, she snorted and filled her lungs with water,

then sank, to the bottom,
and looking down, clear it was, like crystal,

there I saw her.

THE LOVER

What should the young
man say, because he is buying
Modess? Should he

blush or not. Or
turn coyly, his head, to
one side, as if in

the exactitude of his emotion he
were not offended? Were
proud? Of what? To buy

a thing like that.

A COUNTERPOINT

Let me be my own fool
of my own making, the sum of it

is equivocal.
One says of the drunken farmer:

leave him lay off it. And this is
the explanation.

. . . give a man his
I said to her,

manliness: provide
what you want I

creature comfort
want only

for him and herself:
more so. You

preserve essential
think marriage is

hypocrisies—
everything?

in short, make a
Oh well,

home for herself.
I said.

To be in love is like going outside to see what kind of day

it is. Do not
mistake me. If you love

her how prove she
loves also, except that it

occurs, a remote chance on
which you stake

yourself? But barter for
the Indian was a means of sustenance.

There are records.

THE DISAPPOINTMENT

Had you the eyes of a goat,
they would be almond, half-green, half-

yellow, an almond
shape to them. Were you

less as you are, cat-like, a brush
head, sad, sad, un-

goatlike.

THE WARNING

For love—I would
split open your head and put
a candle in
behind the eyes.

Love is dead in us
if we forget
the virtues of an amulet
and quick surprise.

A FORM OF ADAPTATION

My enemies came to get me,
among them a beautiful woman.

And—god, I thought, this will be the end of me,
because I have no resistance.

Taking their part against me even,
flattered that they were concerned,

I lay down before them and looked up soulfully,
thinking perhaps that might help.

And she bent over me to look at me then,
being a woman.

They are wise to send their strongest first, I thought.
And I kissed her.

And they watched her and both of us carefully,
not at all to be tricked.

But how account for love, even if you look for it?
I trusted it.

Were I myself more blithe,
more the gay cavalier,
I would sit on a chair
and blow bubbles into the air.

I would tear up all the checks
made out to me,
not giving a good goddamn
what the hell happened.

I would marry a very rich woman
who had no use for stoves,
and send my present wife
all her old clothes.

And see my present children
on Mondays and Thursdays
and give them chocolate
to be nicer to me.

If being the word
as it was reported—
desperate perhaps, and even foolish,
but god knows useful.

NAUGHTY BOY

When he brings home a whale,
she laughs and says, that's not for real.

And if he won the Irish sweepstakes,
she would say, where were you last night?

Where are you now, for that matter? Am
I always (she says) to be looking

at you? She says,
if I thought it would get any better I

would shoot you, you
nut, you. Then pats her hair

into place, and waits
for Uncle Jim's deep-fired, all-fat, real gone

whale steaks.

LIKE THEY SAY

Underneath the tree on some
soft grass I sat, I

watched two happy
woodpeckers be dis-

turbed by my presence. And
why not, I thought to

myself, why
not.

LA NOCHE

In the court-
yard at midnight, at

midnight. The moon is
locked in itself, to

a man a
familiar thing.

THE WHIP

I spent a night turning in bed,
my love was a feather, a flat

sleeping thing. She was
very white

and quiet, and above us on
the roof, there was another woman I

also loved, had
addressed myself to in

a fit she
returned. That

encompasses it. But now I was
lonely, I yelled,

but what is that? Ugh,
she said, beside me, she put

her hand on
my back, for which act

I think to say this
wrongly.

ALL THAT IS LOVELY IN MEN

Nothing for a dirty man
but soap in his bathtub, a

greasy hand, lover's
nuts

perhaps. Or else

something like sand
with which to scour him

for all
that is lovely in women.

2 1956 - 1958

JUGGLER'S THOUGHT

for my son, David

> Heads up to the sky
> people are walking by
>
> in the land with no heads
> tails hanging to trees
>
> where truth is like an apple
> reddened by frost and sun, and the green
>
> fields go out and out
> under the sun.

A FORM OF WOMEN

I have come far enough
from where I was not before
to have seen the things
looking in at me through the open door

and have walked tonight
by myself
to see the moonlight
and see it as trees

and shapes more fearful
because I feared
what I did not know
but have wanted to know.

My face is my own, I thought.
But you have seen it
turn into a thousand years.
I watched you cry.

I could not touch you.
I wanted very much to
touch you
but could not.

If it is dark
when this is given to you,
have care for its content
when the moon shines.

My face is my own.
My hands are my own.
My mouth is my own
but I am not.

Moon, moon,
when you leave me alone
all the darkness is
an utter blackness,

a pit of fear,
a stench,
hands unreasonable
never to touch.

But I love you.
Do you love me.
What to say
when you see me.

THEY SAY

Up and down
what falls
goes slower and slower
combing her hair.

She is the lovely stranger
who married the forest ranger,
the duck and the dog,
and never was seen again.

THE FRIEND

What I saw in his head
was an inverted vision,
and the glass cracked
when I put my hand in.

My own head is round
with hair for adornment,
but the face
is an ornament.

Your face is wide
with long hair, and eyes
so wide they grow
deep as I watch.

If the world
could only be rounder,
like your head, like mine,
with your eyes for real lakes!

I sleep in myself.
That man was a friend,
sans canoe,
and I wanted to help him.

PLEASE

for James Broughton

> Oh god, let's go.
> This is a poem for Kenneth Patchen.
> Everywhere they are shooting people.
> People people people people.
> This is a poem for Allen Ginsberg.
> I want to be elsewhere, elsewhere.
> This is a poem about a horse that got tired.
> Poor. Old. Tired. Horse.
> I want to go home.
> I want you to go home.
> This is a poem which tells the story,
> which is the story.
> I don't know. I get lost
> If only they would stand still and let me.
> Are you happy, sad, not happy, please come.
> This is a poem for everyone.

THE THREE LADIES

I dreamt. I saw three ladies in a tree,
and the one that I saw most clearly
showed her favors unto me,
and I saw up her leg above the knee!

But when the time for love was come,
and of readiness I had made myself,
upon my head and shoulders
dropped the other two like an unquiet dew.

What were these two but the one?
I saw in their faces, I heard in their words,
wonder of wonders! it was the undoing of me
they came down to see!

Sister, they said to her who upon my lap
sat complacent, expectant:
he is dead in his head, and we
have errands, have errands . . .

Oh song of wistful night! Light shows
where it stops nobody knows, and two
are one, and three, to me, and to look
is not to read the book.

Oh one, two, three! Oh one, two, three!
Three old ladies sat in a tree.

OH NO

If you wander far enough
you will come to it
and when you get there
they will give you a place to sit

for yourself only, in a nice chair,
and all your friends will be there
with smiles on their faces
and they will likewise all have places.

GOODBYE

She stood at the window. There was
a sound, a light.
She stood at the window. A face.

Was it that she was looking for,
he thought. Was it that
she was looking for. He said,

turn from it, turn
from it. The pain is
not unpainful. Turn from it.

The act of her anger, of
the anger she felt then,
not turning to him.

Light eyes would have been more fortunate.
They have cares like store windows.
All the water was shut off,
and winter settled in the house.

The first week they wrote a letter.
He wrote it.
She thought about it.
Peace was in the house like a broken staircase.

I was neat about it, she later wrote
to a relative in Spokane.
She spoke in accents low
as she told me.

A WICKER BASKET

Comes the time when it's later
and onto your table the headwaiter
puts the bill, and very soon after
rings out the sound of lively laughter—

Picking up change, hands like a walrus,
and a face like a barndoor's,
and a head without any apparent size,
nothing but two eyes—

So that's you, man,
or me. I make it as I can,
I pick up, I go
faster than they know—

Out the door, the street like a night,
any night, and no one in sight,
but then, well, there she is,
old friend Liz—

And she opens the door of her cadillac,
I step in back,
and we're gone.
She turns me on—

There are very huge stars, man, in the sky,
and from somewhere very far off someone hands me a slice of
          apple pie,
with a gob of white, white ice cream on top of it,
and I eat it—

Slowly. And while certainly
they are laughing at me, and all around me is racket
of these cats not making it, I make it

in my wicker basket.

THE BED

She walks in beauty like a lake
and eats her steak
with fork and knife
and proves a proper wife.

Her room and board
he can afford, he has made friends
of common pains
and meets his ends.

Oh god, decry
such common finery as puts the need
before the bed, makes true what is
the lie indeed.

JUST FRIENDS

Out of the table endlessly rocking,
sea-shells, and firm,
I saw a face appear
which called me dear.

To be loved is half the battle
I thought.
To be
is to be better than is not.

Now when you are old what will you say?
You don't say,
she said.
That was on a Thursday.

Friday night I left
and haven't been back since.
Everything is water
if you look long enough.

THE WIND

Whatever is to become of me
becomes daily as the acquaintance
with facts is made less the point,
and firm feelings are reencountered.

This morning I drank coffee and orange juice,
waiting for the biscuits which never came.
It is my own failing
because I cannot make them.

Praise god in women.
Give thanks to love in homes.
Without them all men
would starve to the bone.

Mother was helpful but essentially mistaken.
It is the second half of the 20th century.
I screamed that endlessly,
hearing it back distorted.

Who comes?
The light footsteps
down the hall
betoken

—in all her loveliness,
in all her grimness,
in all her asking and staying silent,
all mothers or potentials thereof.

There is no hymn yet written
that could
provoke beyond the laughter I feel
an occasion for this song—

But as love is long-winded,
the moving wind
describes its moving colors
of sound and flight.

AIR: "CAT BIRD SINGING"

Cat bird singing
makes music like sounds coming

at night. The trees, goddamn them,
are huge eyes. They

watch, certainly, what
else should they do? My love

is a person of rare refinement,
and when she speaks,

there is another air,
melody—what Campion spoke of

with his
follow thy fair sunne unhappie shadow . . .

Catbird, catbird.
O lady hear me. I have no

other
voice left.

THE HERO

Each voice which was asked
spoke its words, and heard
more than that, the fair question,
the onerous burden of the asking.

And so the hero, the
hero! stepped that gracefully
into his redemption, losing
or gaining life thereby.

Now we, now I
ask also, and burdened,
tied down, return
and seek the forest also.

Go forth, go forth,
saith the grandmother, the fire
of that old form, and turns
away from the form.

And the forest is dark,
mist hides it, trees
are dim, but I turn
to my father in the dark.

A spark, that spark of hope
which was burned out long ago,
the tedious echo
of the father image

—which only women bear,
also wear, old men, old cares,
and turn, and again find
the disorder in the mind.

Night is dark like the mind,
my mind is dark like the night.
O light the light! Old
foibles of the right.

Into that pit, now pit of
anywhere, the tears upon your hands,
how can you stand
it, I also turn.

I wear the face, I face
the right, the night, the way,
I go along the path
into the last and only dark,

hearing hero! hero!
a voice faint enough, a spark,
a glimmer grown dimmer through years
of old, old fears.

THE WAY

My love's manners in bed
are not to be discussed by me,
as mine by her
I would not credit comment upon gracefully.

Yet I ride by the margin of that lake in
the wood, the castle,
and the excitement of strongholds;
and have a small boy's notion of doing good.

Oh well, I will say here,
knowing each man,
let you find a good wife too,
and love her as hard as you can.

THE TRAVELLER

Into the forest again
whence all roads depend
this way and that
to lead him back.

Upon his shoulders
he places boulders,
upon his eye
the high wide sky.

The first retainer
he gave to her
was a golden
wedding ring.

The second—late at night
he woke up,
leaned over on an elbow,
and kissed her.

The third and the last—
he died with
and gave up loving
and lived with her.

SHE WENT TO STAY

> Trying to chop mother down is like
> hunting deer inside Russia
> with phalangists for hat-pins.
> I couldn't.

A FOLK SONG

for Phil

> Hitch up honey for the
> market race all
> the way to the plaza!
>
> If she don't run you
> can push her like
> hell. I know.

BALLAD OF THE DESPAIRING HUSBAND

My wife and I lived all alone,
contention was our only bone.
I fought with her, she fought with me,
and things went on right merrily.

But now I live here by myself
with hardly a damn thing on the shelf,
and pass my days with little cheer
since I have parted from my dear.

Oh come home soon, I write to her.
Go fuck yourself, is her answer.
Now what is that, for Christian word?
I hope she feeds on dried goose turd.

But still I love her, yes I do.
I love her and the children too.
I only think it fit that she
should quickly come right back to me.

Ah no, she says, and she is tough,
and smacks me down with her rebuff.
Ah no, she says, I will not come
after the bloody things you've done.

Oh wife, oh wife—I tell you true,
I never loved no one but you.
I never will, it cannot be
another woman is for me.

That may be right, she will say then,
but as for me, there's other men.
And I will tell you I propose
to catch them firmly by the nose.

And I will wear what dresses I choose!
And I will dance, and what's to lose!
I'm free of you, you little prick,
and I'm the one can make it stick.

Was this the darling I did love?
Was this that mercy from above
did open violets in the spring—
and made my own worn self to sing?

She was. I know. And she is still,
and if I love her? then so I will.
And I will tell her, and tell her right . . .

Oh lovely lady, morning or evening or afternoon.
Oh lovely lady, eating with or without a spoon.
Oh most lovely lady, whether dressed or undressed or partly.
Oh most lovely lady, getting up or going to bed or sitting only.

Oh loveliest of ladies, than whom none is more fair, more
            gracious, more beautiful.
Oh loveliest of ladies, whether you are just or unjust,
            merciful, indifferent, or cruel.
Oh most loveliest of ladies, doing whatever, seeing whatever,
            being whatever.
Oh most loveliest of ladies, in rain, in shine, in any weather.

Oh lady, grant me time,
please, to finish my rhyme.

DAMON & PYTHIAS

When he got into bed,
he was dead.

Oh god, god, god, he said.
She watched him take off his shoes

and kneel there
to look for the change which had fallen

out of his pocket.
Old Mr. Jones

whom nobody loves
went to market for it,

and almost found it
under a table,

but by that time was unable.
And the other day two men,

who had been known as friends,
were said to be living together again.

If you were going to get a pet
what kind of animal would you get.

A soft bodied dog, a hen—
feathers and fur to begin it again.

When the sun goes down and it gets dark
I saw an animal in a park.

Bring it home, to give it to you.
I have seen animals break in two.

You were hoping for something soft
and loyal and clean and wondrously careful—

a form of otherwise vicious habit
can have long ears and be called a rabbit.

Dead. Died. Will die. Want.
Morning, midnight. I asked you

if you were going to get a pet
what kind of animal would you get.

THE TUNNEL

Tonight, nothing is long enough—
time isn't.
Were there a fire,
it would burn now.

Were there a heaven,
I would have gone long ago.
I think that light
is the final image.

But time reoccurs,
love—and an echo.
A time passes
love in the dark.

THE SAINTS

Heaven won't have to do with its multitudes.
There isn't room enough.
A thought we've all had perhaps,
now taken beyond that consideration.

Last night I saw several people
in a dream, in shapes
of all of this: faces and hands,
and things to say, too.

I love you, one said.
And I love you too. Let's
get out of this.
One said: I have to take a piss.

The door to the pantry was dark,
where the two crouched,
his hand on her back, her hand
on his back. I looked

at an evil, in the face.
I saw its place, in the universe,
and laughed back
until my mind cracked.

THE NAMES

When they came near,
the one, two, three, four,
all five of us sat
in the broken seat.

Oh glad to see,
oh glad to be,
where company
is so derived
from sticks and stones,
bottles and bones.

A GIFT OF GREAT VALUE

Oh that horse I see so high
when the world shrinks into its
relationships, my mother
sees as well as I.

She was born, but I bore with her.
This horse was a mighty occasion!
The intensity of its feet! The height
of its immense body!

Now then in wonder at evening, at
the last small entrance of the night,
my mother calls it, and I
call it my father.

With angry face, with no
rights, with impetuosity and
sterile vision—and a great
wind we ride.

MY LOVE

It falleth like a stick.
  It lieth like air.
It is wonderment and bewilderment,
  to test true.

It is no thing, but of two,
  equal: as the mind turns to it,
it doubleth,
  as one alone.

Where it is, there is
  everywhere, separate,
yet few—as dew
  to night is.

SATURDAY AFTERNOON

It is like a monster come to dinner,
and the dinner table is set,
the fire in the fireplace,
good luck to good humor—

The monster you love is home again,
and he tells you the stories of the world,
big cities, small men
and women.

Make room for the furry, wooden eyed
monster. He is my friend
whom you burn.
Amen.

THE INVOICE

I once wrote a letter as follows:
dear Jim, I would like to borrow
200 dollars from you
to see me through.

I also wrote another: dearest M/
please come.
There is no one
here at all.

I got word today,
viz: hey
sport, how are you making it?
And, why don't you get with it.

SOMEWHERE

The galloping collection of boards
are the house which I afforded
one evening to walk into
just as the night came down.

Dark inside, the candle
lit of its own free will, the attic
groaned then, the stairs
led me up into the air.

From outside, it must have seemed
a wonder that it was
the inside he as me saw
in the dark there.

The end of the year wears its face in the moon against the
    disguises one would otherwise put upon it.
It is the mild temper of midnight that embarrasses us and oh!
    we turn away into reassuring daylight but backwards.

If it were the forward motion one wanted—
What tempers would not be resolved, can one keep the night
    out of it as or when it was there?

Darling (she had gone) we speak as if there never were an
    answer.
We speak (to the back, to sleep, to heads). We are alone in the
    new minute, hour, or year, or nowhere.

House. Your hand is too far from me. Tree, speak. The moon is
    white in the branches, the night is white in the mind of it.
Love, tell me the time. What time is it? The second, the moment
    moving in the moon?

Of the strangeness of bending backwards until the mind is an
    instant of mind in the moon's light white upon an
Endless black desert, the sand, in the night of the last moment
    of the year.

God give you pardon from gratitude
and other mild forms of servitude—

and make peace for all of us
with what is easy.

LADY BIRD

A lady asks me
and I would tell

what is it
she has found the burden of.

To be happy
now she cries, and all things

turn backward
and impossible.

God knows that I love her,
and would comfort her—

but the invention is
a parallel sufferance.

Mine for hers,
hers for mine.

FOR A FRIEND

Who remembers him also, he thinks
(but to himself and as himself).

Himself alone is dominant
in a world of no one else.

ENTRE NOUS

If I can't hope then to hell with it.
I don't want to live like this?

Like this, he said. Where were you?
She was around in back of the bureau

where he pushed her?
Hell no, she just fell.

I sing the song of the sleeping wife,
who married to sleep,
who would not sleep simply to get married;

who can be up at dawn, yet
never cannot go to sleep if there is
good reason not to go to sleep;

who sleeps to sleep,
who has no other purpose in mind,
who wouldn't even hear you if you asked her.

A pretty party for people
to become engaged in, she was

twentythree, he
was a hundred and twentyseven times

all the times, over and over
and under and under she went

down stairs, through doorways,
glass, alabaster, an iron shovel

stood waiting and
she lifted it to dig

back
and back to mother,

father and brother,
grandfather and grandmother—

They are all dead now.

HEROES

In all those stories the hero
is beyond himself into the next
thing, be it those labors
of Hercules, or Aeneas going into death.

I thought the instant of the one humanness
in Virgil's plan of it
was that it was of course human enough to die,
yet to come back, as he said, *hoc opus, hic labor est.*

That was the Cumaean Sibyl speaking.
This is Robert Creeley, and Virgil
is dead now two thousand years, yet Hercules
and the *Aeneid*, yet all that industrious wis-

dom lives in the way the mountains
and the desert are waiting
for the heroes, and death also
can still propose the old labors.

That dim shattering character of nerves
which creates faces in the dark
speaks of the heaven and hell
as a form of corporate existence.

Oh don't say it isn't so,
think to understand if
the last time you looked
you were still a man.

It is a viscous form of self-
propulsion that lets the feet grip
the floor, as the head
lifts to the door,

lurches, ghostwise, out, and to
the window to fall through,
yet closes it to let
the cat out too.

After that, silence, silence.
On the floor the hands
find quiet, the mouth goes lax.
Oh! Look forward to get back.

Oh wisdom to find fault with
what is after all a plan.

THE FLOWER

I think I grow tensions
like flowers
in a wood where
nobody goes.

Each wound is perfect,
encloses itself in a tiny
imperceptible blossom,
making pain.

Pain is a flower like that one,
like this one,
like that one,
like this one.

THE LETTER

I did not expect you
to stay married to
one man all your life,
no matter you were his wife.

I thought the pain was endless—
but the form existent,
as it is form,
and as such I loved it.

I loved you as well
even as you might tell,
giving evidence
as to how much was penitence.

What is the form is the gro-
tesquerie—the accident
of the moon's light
on your face.

Oh love, an empty table!
An empty bottle also.
But no trick will go
so far but not further.

The end of the year is a div-
ision, a drunken derision
of composition's accident.
We both fell.

I fell. You fell.
In hell we will tell of it.
Form's accidents, we move back-
wards to love . . .

The movement of the
sentence tells me of you
as it was the bottle we drank?
No. It was no accident.

Agh, form is what happens?
Form is an accompaniment.
I to love, you to love:
syntactic accident.

It will all come true,
in a year.
The empty bottle, the empty table,
tell where we were.

THE SOUVENIR

Passing into the wilderness of twisted trees,
below the goats and sheep look up at us,
as we climb the hill for our picnic
years ago.

From something in the trees
looking down at me

or else an inexact sign
of a remote and artificial tenderness—

a woman who passes me
and who will not consider me—

things I have tried to take
with which to make something

like a toy for my children
and a story to be quietly forgotten.

Oh God, send me an omen
that I may remember more often.

Keep me, see to me,
let me look.

Being unsure, there is the fate
of doing nothing right.

THE DOOR

for Robert Duncan

It is hard going to the door
cut so small in the wall where
the vision which echoes loneliness
brings a scent of wild flowers in a wood.

What I understood, I understand.
My mind is sometime torment,
sometimes good and filled with livelihood,
and feels the ground.

But I see the door,
and knew the wall, and wanted the wood,
and would get there if I could
with my feet and hands and mind.

Lady, do not banish me
for digressions. My nature
is a quagmire of unresolved
confessions. Lady, I follow.

I walked away from myself,
I left the room, I found the garden,
I knew the woman
in it, together we lay down.

Dead night remembers. In December
we change, not multiplied but dispersed,
sneaked out of childhood,
the ritual of dismemberment.

Mighty magic is a mother,
in her there is another issue

of fixture, repeated form, the race renewal,
the charge of the command.

The garden echoes across the room.
It is fixed in the wall like a mirror
that faces a window behind you
and reflects the shadows.

May I go now?
Am I allowed to bow myself down
in the ridiculous posture of renewal,
of the insistence of which I am the virtue?

Nothing for You is untoward.
Inside You would also be tall,
more tall, more beautiful.
Come toward me from the wall, I want to be with You.

So I screamed to You,
who hears as the wind, and changes
multiply, invariably,
changes in the mind.

Running to the door, I ran down
as a clock runs down. Walked backwards,
stumbled, sat down
hard on the floor near the wall.

Where were You.
How absurd, how vicious.
There is nothing to do but get up.
My knees were iron, I rusted in worship, of You.

For that one sings, one
writes the spring poem, one goes on walking.
The Lady has always moved to the next town
and you stumble on after Her.

The door in the wall leads to the garden
where in the sunlight sit
the Graces in long Victorian dresses,
of which my grandmother had spoken.

History sings in their faces.
They are young, they are obtainable,
and you follow after them also
in the service of God and Truth.

But the Lady is indefinable,
she will be the door in the wall
to the garden in sunlight.
I will go on talking forever.

I will never get there.
Oh Lady, remember me
who in Your service grows older
not wiser, no more than before.

How can I die alone.
Where will I be then who am now alone,
what groans so pathetically
in this room where I am alone?

I will go to the garden.
I will be a romantic, I will sell.
myself in hell,
in heaven also I will be.

In my mind I see the door,
I see the sunlight before me across the floor
beckon to me, as the Lady's skirt
moves small beyond it.

THE HILL

It is sometime since I have been
to what it was had once turned me backwards,
and made my head into
a cruel instrument.

It is simple
to confess. Then done,
to walk away, walk away,
to come again.

But that form, I must answer,
is dead in me, completely,
and I will not allow it
to reappear—

Saith perversity, the willful,
the magnanimous cruelty,
which is in me
like a hill.

3 ~1959 - 1960~

THE AWAKENING

for Charles Olson

He feels small as he awakens,
but in the stream's sudden mirror,
a pool of darkening water,
sees his size with his own two eyes.

The trees are taller here,
fall off to no field or clearing,
and depend on the inswept air
for the place in which he finds himself thus lost.

I was going on to tell you
when the door bell rang it was
another story as I know
previously had happened, had occurred.

That was a woman's impression
of the wonders of the morning, the same place,
whiter air now, and strong breezes
move the birds off in that first freshening.

O wisest of gods! Unnatural prerogatives
would err to concur, would fall deafened
between the seen, the green green,
and the ring of a far off telephone.

God is no bone of whitened contention.
God is not air, nor hair, is not
a conclusive concluding
to remote yearnings. He moves

only as I move, you also move to
the awakening, across long rows, of beds,
stumble breathlessly, on leg pins and crutch,
moving at all as all men, because you must.

As I was walking
  I came upon
chance walking
  the same road upon.

As I sat down
  by chance to move
later
  if and as I might,

light the wood was,
  light and green,
and what I saw
  before I had not seen.

It was a lady
  accompanied
by goat men
  leading her.

Her hair held earth.
  Her eyes were dark.
A double flute
  made her move.

"O love,
  where are you
leading
  me now?"

THE RAIN

All night the sound had
come back again,
and again falls
this quiet, persistent rain.

What am I to myself
that must be remembered,
insisted upon
so often? Is it

that never the ease,
even the hardness,
of rain falling
will have for me

something other than this,
something not so insistent—
am I to be locked in this
final uneasiness.

Love, if you love me,
lie next to me.
Be for me, like rain,
the getting out

of the tiredness, the fatuousness, the semi-
lust of intentional indifference.
Be wet
with a decent happiness.

THE WOMAN

I called her across the room,
could see that what she stood on
held her up, and now she came
as if she moved in time.

In time to what she moved,
her hands, her hair, her eyes, all things
by which I took her to be there
did come along.

It was not right or wrong
but signally despair, to be about
to speak to her
as if her substance shouted.

MIDNIGHT

When the rain stops
and the cat drops
out of the tree
to walk

away, when the rain stops,
when the others come home, when
the phone stops,
the drip of water, the

potential of a caller
any Sunday afternoon.

THE KID

If it falls flat
I'm used to it. Yet
cannot grow when
I can't begin again.

Nowise to secure
what's left to others. They
forget.
But I remember.

How carelessly ease falls
around me! All the trees
have it, the leaves
all green!

I want to grow in ground too,
want it to come true
what they said about if you planted
the acorn the tree would grow.

LADY IN BLACK

The mental picture which the
lady in black if she be
coming, or going,
offered by the occasion

to the church, behind the
black car, lately
stepped out of, and
her dress

falls, lets
all eyes as if
people were
looking

see
her still
an attitude
perplexing.

THE PLAN

Daytime
wonder at
the quieter possibilities
of slumber,

deep sleep,
in peace
some place the mind
will yet escape.

Or else, truth,
the mind
this time at last
trapped:

no voice, no
way left. The
hand at last
can tighten.

Why live
in the middle
of this
damned muddle?

Why not—
lesser thing?
find out
what another will bring.

Woman, addressed,
speaks easily
unless
she is depressed.

Children, wiser,
make their own
things unless
thrown under

the way, the way
it was yesterday, will
be also today
and tomorrow.

THE JOKE

There was a joke
went on a walk like
over the hill, and there before them
these weary travellers
saw valleys and farms
of muscles, tits raised high
in the sky of their vision which bewildered
them. They were
no ordinary men but those who come
innocent, late and alone
to women and a home, and keep on talking
and keep on walking.

THE SONG

It still makes sense
to know the song after all.

My wiseness I wear
in despair of something better.

I am all beggar,
I am all ears.

Soon everything will be sold
and I can go back home

by myself again
and try to be a man.

THE BIRD

What did you say to me
   that I had not heard.
She said she saw
   a small bird.

Where was it.
   In a tree.
Ah, he said, I thought
   you spoke to me.

YELLOW

He wants to be an Indian,
someone else a white man,
or black man, pacing
this to a reason simply given.

What do they put in the graves of
dissatisfied men?
What for the women
who denied them, changing

their colors into
greens, reds, blues,
yellow. Her hands were
yellow, her eyes were

yellow. The Indians want
her to be their queen
because she is such a
lovely color.

THE CRACKS

Don't step
so lightly. Break
your back, missed
the step. Don't go

away mad, lady in
the nightmare. You
are central,
even necessary.

I will attempt to describe you.
I will be completely without
face, a lost
chance, nothing at all left.

"Well," he said
as he was leaving,
"blood
tells."

But you remembered quickly
other times, other faces,
and I slipped between the good
intentions, breathlessly.

What a good boy am I who
wants to. Will you,
mother, come quickly,
won't you. Why not

go quietly, be left
with a memory
or an insinuation or two
of cracks in a pavement.

JACK'S BLUES

I'm going to roll up
a monkey and smoke it, put
an elephant in the pot. I'm going out
and never come back.

What's better than that.
Lying on your back, flat
on your back with your
eyes to the view.

Oh the view is blue, I saw that
too, yesterday and you,
red eyes and blue,
funked.

I'm going to roll up
a rug and smoke it, put
the car in the garage and I'm
gone, like a sad old candle.

OUT OF SIGHT

He thinks
always things
will be simpler,
with face

of a clown
so that the mouth
rolls down, then
the eye shuts

as a fist
to hold patience,
patience,
in the locked mind.

A TOKEN

My lady
fair with
soft
arms, what

can I say to
you—words, words
as if all
worlds were there.

THE MAN

He hie fie finger
speak in simple sound
feels much better
lying down.

He toes is broken
all he foot go
rotten
now. He look

he hurt bad, see
danger all around he
no see before
come down on him.

THE MEMORY

Like a river she was,
huge roily mass of water
carrying tree trunks
and divers drunks.

Like a Priscilla, a feminine Benjamin,
a whore gone right over
the falls,
she was.

Did you know her.
Did you love her, brother.
Did wonder pour down
on the whole goddamn town.

TO AND

To and
back and forth,
direction
is a third

or simple fourth
of the intention
like it
goes and goes.

No
more snow this
winter?
No more snow.

Then what replaces
all the faces,
wasted,
wasted.

A WISH

So much rain
to make the mud again,
trees green
and flowers also.

The water which
ran up the sun
and down again,
it is the same.

A man of supple
yielding manner
might, too, discover
ways of water.

SONG

What I took in my hand
grew in weight. You must
understand it
was not obscene.

Night comes. We sleep.
Then if you know what
say it.
Don't pretend.

Guises are
what enemies wear. You
and I live
in a prayer.

Helpless. Helpless,
should I speak.
Would you.
What do you think of me.

No woman ever was,
was wiser
than you. None is
more true.

But fate, love, fate
scares me. What
I took in my hand
grows in weight.

The quieter the people are
the slower the time passes

until there is a solitary man
sitting in the figure of silence.

Then scream at him,
come here you idiot it's going to go off.

A face that is no face
but the features, of a face, pasted

on a face until that face
is faceless, answers by

a being nothing there
where there was a man.

NOT NOW

I can see you,
hairy, extended, vulnerable,
but how did you get up there.
Where were you going all alone,

why didn't you wait
for the others to come home
to go too, they would
have gone with you.

THE TIME

They walk in and fall into
the large crack in the floor
with the room upended on side
to make the floor a wall.

Upwards or downwards now
they fall into the crack,
having no floor
or ceiling to refer to,

what time comes to,
the place it all goes into.
All that was an instant ago
is gone now.

SONG

Those rivers run from that land
to sea. The wind
finds trees to move,
then goes again.

And me, why me
on any day might be
favored with kind prosperity
or sunk in wretched misery.

I cannot stop the weather
by putting together
myself and another
to stop those rivers.

Or hold the wind
with my hand from the tree,
the mind from the thing,
love from her or me.

Be natural, while alive.
Dead, we die to that
also, and go another
course, I hope.

And me, why me
on any day might be
favored with kind prosperity
or sunk in wretched misery.

You I want back of me
in the life we have here,
waiting to see
what becomes of it.

Call, call loud,
I will hear you, or if
not me, the wind will
for the sake of the tree.

THE RESCUE

The man sits in a timelessness
with the horse under him in time
to a movement of legs and hooves
upon a timeless sand.

Distance comes in from the foreground
present in the picture as time
he reads outward from
and comes from that beginning.

A wind blows in
and out and all about the man
as the horse ran
and runs to come in time.

A house is burning in the sand.
A man and horse are burning.
The wind is burning.
They are running to arrive.

THE PARADOX

Looking down at her
long hair,
we saw the position
in which we placed her.

Yet our own
a formula, the street
she walked up
she looked down on.

THE END OF THE DAY

Oh who is
so cosy with
despair and
all, they will

not come
rejuvenated, to
the last spectacle
of the day. Look!

the sun is
sinking, now
it's
gone. Night,

good and sweet
night, good
night, good, good
night, has come.

"What he holds to
        is a cross
and by just that much
        is his load increased."

*

"Yet the eyes
        cannot die in a face
whereof the hands
        are nailed in place."

*

"I wish I might grow
        tall like a tree
to be cut down
        to bear such beauty."

For fear I want
to make myself again
under the thumb
of old love, old time

subservience
and pain, bent
into a nail that will
not come out.

Why, love, does it
make such a difference
not to be heard
in spite of self

or what we may feel,
one for the other,
but as a hammer
to drive again

bent nail
into old hurt?

THE GIFT

He hands
down the gift
as from a great
height, his

precious
understanding clothed
in miraculous
fortitude. This

is the present
of the ages, all
rewards
in itself.

But the lady—
she disdain-
ful, all
in white for

this occasion—cries
out petulantly, is
that all, is
that all.

THE HOUSE

for Louis Zukofsky

Mud put
upon mud,
lifted
to make room,

house
a cave,
and
colder night.

To sleep
in, live in,
to come in
from heat,

all form derived
from kind,
built
with that in mind.

YOUNG WOMAN

Young woman, older
woman, as soon as the
words begin, you
leave, rightly.

How pace yourself behind,
how follow when it is you
also who leads, to be
followed, and why not.

Is there a patience
we learn, barely, hardly,
a condition into which we
are suspended?

Is there a place for us,
do you know it well
enough that without thought
it can be found?

I think, and
therefore I am not,
who was to have been, as you,
something else.

THE POOL

My embarrassment at his nakedness,
at the pool's edge,
and my wife, with his,
standing, watching—

this was a freedom
not given me who am
more naked,
less contained

by my own white flesh
and the ability
to take quietly
what comes to me.

The sense of myself
separate, grew
a white mirror
in the quiet water

he breaks with his hands
and feet, kicking,
pulls up to land
on the edge by the feet

of these women
who must know
that for each
man is a speech

describes him, makes
the day grow white
and sure, a quietness of water
in the mind,

lets hang, descriptive
as a risk, something
for which he cannot find
a means or time.

The love of a woman
is the possibility which
surrounds her as hair
her head, as the love of her

follows and describes
her. But what if
they die, then there is
still the aura

left, left sadly, but
hovers in the air, surely,
where this had taken place?
Then sing, of her, of whom

it will be said, he
sang of her, it was the
song he made which made her
happy, so she lived.

MIND'S HEART

Mind's heart, it must
be that some
truth lies locked
in you.

Or else, lies, all
lies, and no man
true enough to know
the difference.

THE NAME

Be natural
wise
as you can be,
my daughter,

let my name
be in you flesh
I gave you
in the act of

loving your mother,
all your days
her ways,
the woman in you

brought from
sensuality's measure,
no other,
there was no thought

of it but such
pleasure all women
must be in her,
as you. But not wiser,

not more of nature
than her hair,
the eyes
she gives you.

There will not be another
woman such as you
are. Remember
your mother,

the way you came,
the days of waiting.
Be natural,
daughter, wise

as you can be,
all my daughters,
be women
for men

when that time comes.
Let the rhetoric
stay with me
your father. Let

me talk about it,
saving you such
vicious self-
exposure, let you

pass it on
in you. I cannot
be more than the man
who watches.

THE FIRST TIME

We are given a chance,
among the worst something left
otherwise, hopeful
circumstance.

As I spoke to you,
once,
I loved you
as simply as that.

Now to go back,
I cannot
but going on,
will not forget the first time

You likewise
with me must be
testament
to pain's indifference.

We are only careful
for such a memory, more
careful, I think,
than we ever thought to be.

THE FIGURES

The stillness
of the wood,
the figures formed

by hands so still
they touched it
to be one

hand holding one
hand, faces
without eyes,

bodies of wooden
stone, so still
they will not move

from that quiet
action ever
again. Did the man

who made them find
a like quiet? In
the act of making them

it must have been
so still he heard the wood
and felt it with his hands

moving into
the forms
he has given to them,

one by singular
one, so quiet,
so still.

THE ROSE

for Bobbie

Up and down
she walks, listless
form, a movement
quietly misled.

Now, speak to her.
"Did you want
to go, then why
don't you."

She went. There were
things she left
in the room
as a form of it.

He follows, walking.
Where do they walk now?
Do they talk now
where they are

in that other place
grown monstrous,
quiet quiet air
as breath.

And all about a rosy
mark discloses
her nature
to him, vague and unsure.

There roses, here roses,
flowers, a pose of
nature, her
nature has disclosed to him.

Yet breathing, crouched
in the dark,
he is there
also, recovers,

to bring her back
to herself, himself.
The room wavers,
wavers.

And as if,
as if a cloud had
broken at last
open

and all the rain
from that,
from that had fallen
on them,

on them there is a mark
of her nature, her flowers,
and his room, his nature,
to come home to.

THE EYE

Moon
and clouds, will
we drift

higher
than that we
look at,

moon's and
mind's
eye.

LOVE COMES QUIETLY

Love comes quietly,
finally, drops
about me, on me,
in the old ways.

What did I know
thinking myself
able to go
alone all the way.

Stone,
like stillness,
around you my
mind sits, it is

a proper form
for
it, like
stone, like

compression itself,
fixed fast,
grey,
without a sound.

THE PEOPLE

Wistful,
they speak of
satis-
faction, love

and divers
other
things. It
comforts,

it surprises
them, the
old
remembrances,

like hands to
hold them
safe and
warm. So

must it be, then,
some god looks
truly down
upon them.

THE WIFE

I know two women
    and the one
is tangible substance,
    flesh and bone.

The other in my mind
    occurs.
She keeps her strict
    proportion there.

But how should I
    propose to live
with two such creatures
    in my bed.—

or how shall he
    who has a wife
yield two to one
    and watch the other die.

THE SNOW

The broken snow should leave the traces
of yesterday's walks, the paths worn in,
and bring friends to our door
somewhere in the dark winter.

Sometime in April I will get at last
the flowers promised you long ago,—
to think of it
will help us through.

The night is a pleasure to us,
I think sleeping, and what warmth secures
me you bring,
giving at last freely of yourself.

Myself was old, was confused, was wanting,—
to sing of an old song,
through the last echo of hurting,
brought now home.

Clear smoke,
a fire in the far off
haze of summer,
burning somewhere.

What is
a lonely heart for
if not
for itself alone.

Do the questions
answer themselves,
all wonder
brought to a reckoning?

When you are done,
I am done,
then it seems that
one by one

we can leave it all,
to go on.

For friendship
make a chain that holds,
to be bound to
others, two by two,

a walk, a garland,
handed by hands
that cannot move
unless they hold.

THE GESTURE

The gesture she makes
to rise,
all her flesh is white,
and tired.

Now morning, now
night, and sun
shines as
moonlight.

Sun, for her
make do
light with bright
moon and

love and children
sleeping,
in her tired
mind's keeping.

FOR LOVE

for Bobbie

Yesterday I wanted to
speak of it, that sense above
the others to me
important because all

that I know derives
from what it teaches me.
Today, what is it that
is finally so helpless,

different, despairs of its own
statement, wants to
turn away, endlessly
to turn away.

If the moon did not . . .
no, if you did not
I wouldn't either, but
what would I not

do, what prevention, what
thing so quickly stopped.
That is love yesterday
or tomorrow, not

now. Can I eat
what you give me. I
have not earned it. Must
I think of everything

as earned. Now love also
becomes a reward so
remote from me I have
only made it with my mind.

Here is tedium,
despair, a painful

sense of isolation and
whimsical if pompous

self-regard. But that image
is only of the mind's
vague structure, vague to me
because it is my own.

Love, what do I think
to say. I cannot say it.
What have you become to ask,
what have I made you into,

companion, good company,
crossed legs with skirt, or
soft body under
the bones of the bed.

Nothing says anything
but that which it wishes
would come true, fears
what else might happen in

some other place, some
other time not this one.
A voice in my place, an
echo of that only in yours.

Let me stumble into
not the confession but
the obsession I begin with
now. For you

also (also)
some time beyond place, or
place beyond time, no
mind left to

say anything at all,
that face gone, now.
Into the company of love
it all returns.

4 1961 - 1965

It is all a rhythm,
from the shutting
door, to the window
opening,

the seasons, the sun's
light, the moon,
the oceans, the
growing of things,

the mind in men
personal, recurring
in them again,
thinking the end

is not the end, the
time returning,
themselves dead, but
someone else coming.

If in death I am dead,
then in life also
dying, dying . . .
And the women cry and die.

The little children
grow only to old men.
The grass dries,
the force goes.

But is met by another
returning, oh not mine,
not mine, and
in turn dies.

The rhythm which projects
from itself continuity
bending all to its force
from window to door,
from ceiling to floor,
light at the opening,
dark at the closing.

THE ROCKS

Trying to think of
some way out, the
rocks of thought

which displace,
dropped in
the water,

much else.
So life is
water, love also

has substance of
like kind.
Wanting

water a Sunday
morning God will
not provide

is it my
wife, her warmth
lying

beside me, is
that sense of warm
moistness the condition

in which all grows?
Drop
the rock,

think well, think
well of me.

The sun's
sky in
form of
blue sky
that

water will
never make
even
in
reflection.

Sing, song,
mind's form
feeling
if
mistaken,

shaken,
broken water's
forms, love's
error
in water.

THE MOUNTAINS IN THE DESERT

The mountains blue now
at the back of my head,
such geography of self and soul
brought to such limit of sight,

I cannot relieve it
nor leave it, my mind locked
in seeing it
as the light fades.

Tonight let me go
at last out of whatever
mind I thought to have,
and all the habits of it.

WAITING

He pushes behind the words
which, awkward, catch
and turn him to a disturbed
and fumbling man.

What if it all stops.
Then silence
is as silence was
again.

What if the last time
he was moved to touch,
work out in his own mind,
such limits was the last—

and then a quiet, a dull
space of hanging actions, all
depending on some time
has come and gone.

God help him then
if such things can.
That risk
is all there is.

THE INVITATION

If it ever is
as it will be,
then enough is
enough. They

think in clusters
round the interminable
subject all but
lost to my mind.

Well, here I am,
they say, together.
Or here you are,
them, and it.

Let's build a house of
human pieces, arms
and hair, not telling
any one. Shout

from the feet, face
facts as accumulations,
we can
do it.

Or and, and as
it's done, what flesh
can do, home again
we'll say,

we'll fall down streets
rolling,
balls
of clear substance.

THE TURN

Each way the turn
twists, to be apprehended:
now she is
there, now she

is not, goes, but
did she, having gone,
went before
the eye saw

nothing. The tree
cannot walk, all its
going must
be violence. They listen

to the saw cut, the
roots scream. And in eating
even a stalk of celery
there will be pathetic screaming.

But what we want
is not what we get.
What we saw, we think
we will see again?

We will not. Moving,
we will
move, and then
stop.

FOR W.C.W. (2)

The rhyme is after
all the repeated
insistence.

There, you say, and
there, and there,
and and becomes

just so. And
what one wants is
what one wants,

yet complexly
as you
say.

Let's
let it go.
I want—

Then there is—
and,
I want.

SONG

The grit
of things,
a measure
resistant—

times walk-
ing, talk-
ing, telling
lies and

all the other
places, no
one ever
quite the same.

THE FIRE

Oh flame falling, as shaken, as the stories
my daughter sees in the light, forming, seeing
the simple burning as an action which to speak of
now I complicate, with my own burning, her story.

Then it all goes, saying, here they were, and are,
and will be again, as I used to think, to remember,
then they were here, and now, again, they are.

What in the light's form finds her face,
makes of her eyes the simple grace.

FOR NO CLEAR REASON

I dreamt last night
the fright was over, that
the dust came, and then water,
and women and men, together
again, and all was quiet
in the dim moon's light.

A paean of such patience—
laughing, laughing at me,
and the days extend over
the earth's great cover,
grass, trees, and flower-
ing season, for no clear reason.

THE MESSENGERS

for Allen Ginsberg

The huge dog, Broderick, and
the smile of the quick eyes
of Allen light a kind world.

Their feelings, under some distance
of remote skin, must touch,
wondering at what impatience does

block them. So little love
to share among so many, so much
yellow-orange hair, on the one,

and on the other, such a darkness
of long hanging hair now, such
slightness of body, and a voice that

rises on the sounds of feeling.
Aie! It raises the world, lifts,
falls, like a sudden sunlight, like

that edge of the black night sweeps
the low lying fields, of soft grasses,
bodies, fills them with quiet longing

FOR LESLIE

For you there ought
to be words as something
at least to say

of what couldn't be
then, the whole
sense crowded, almost

a comfortable agony
so full
I felt it.

Two years go,
the same wide sky
sits over us.

There, the grave is
I cannot
even go to

under some trees
in the grass
of someone's cemetery.

What argument can be
used now, the light so
strikes in,

so blonde you are,
so different from our darkness,
your eyes such blue.

"is the grandson
of Thomas L. Creeley, who acquired
eight acres of Belmont land around 1880 and

continued

"His house was numbered 375
Common st.

and his farm lands,
through the heart of which the present Creeley
rd. runs, adjoined

the Chenery holdings and extended
toward Waverly from upper
Common st.
                The author's father, the late
Dr. Oscar Creeley,
was a prominent Watertown physician
for many years
                and headed
the staff of Symmes Hospital in Arlington."

I, is late

But I saw a picture of him once, T.L.
in a chair in Belmont, or it was his invalid
and patient wife they told me sat there, he
was standing, long and steady faced,
a burden to him she was, and the son. The
other child had died

They waited, so my father
who also died when I is four gave all
to something like
the word 'adjoined', 'extended'
so I feels

I sees the time as long and wavering
grass in all about the lot in all that
cemetery again the old man owned a part of
so they couldn't dig him up.

SOMETHING

I approach with such
a careful tremor, always
I feel the finally foolish

question of how it is,
then, supposed to be felt,
and by whom. I remember

once in a rented room on
27th street, the woman I loved
then, literally, after we

had made love on the large
bed sitting across from
a basin with two faucets, she

had to pee but was nervous,
embarrassed I suppose I
would watch her who had but

a moment ago been completely
open to me, naked, on
the same bed. Squatting, her

head reflected in the mirror,
the hair dark there, the
full of her face, the shoulders,

sat spread-legged, turned on
one faucet and shyly pissed. What
love might learn from such a sight.

WALKING

                    In my head I am
                    walking but I am not
                    in my head, where

                    is there to walk,
                    not thought of, is
                    the road itself more

                    than seen. I think
                    it might be, feel
                    as my feet do, and

                    continue, and
                    at last reach, slowly,
                    one end of my intention.

Locate I
love you some-
where in

teeth and
eyes, bite
it but

take care not
to hurt, you
want so

much so
little. Words
say everything,

I
love you
again,

then what
is emptiness
for. To

fill, fill.
I heard words
and words full

of holes
aching. Speech
is a mouth.

THE WINDOW

Position is where you
put it, where it is,
did you, for example, that

large tank there, silvered,
with the white church along-
side, lift

all that, to what
purpose? How
heavy the slow

world is with
everything put
in place. Some

man walks by, a
car beside him on
the dropped

road, a leaf of
yellow color is
going to

fall. It
all drops into
place. My

face is heavy
with the sight. I can
feel my eye breaking.

THE CHANCE

For whatever, it could
be done, simply
remove it, cut the

offending member. Once
in a photograph by
Frederick Sommer a leg

lay on what was apparently
black velvet cut
from its attachment

to the rest, the foot
showing the incised
wound whereof

the beauty
of all
reasons.

HELLO

With a quick
jump he caught
the edge of

her eye and
it tore, down,
ripping. She

shuddered,
with the unexpected
assault, but

to his vantage
he held by
what flesh was left.

More gaily, dance
with such ladies make
a circumstance of dancing.

Let them lead
around and around, all
awkwardness apart.

There is
an easy grace gained
from falling forward

in time, in
simple time to
all their graces.

There is love only
as love is. These
senses recreate
their definition—a hand

holds within itself
all reason. The eyes
have seen such
beauty they close.

But continue. So the voice
again, *these senses recreate*
their singular condition
felt, and felt again.

I hear. I hear
the mind close, the voice
go on beyond it,
the hands open.

Hard, they hold so
closely themselves, only,
empty grasping of
such sensation.

Hear, there where
the echoes are
louder, clearer,
senses of sound

opening and closing,
no longer love's
only, mind's intention,
eyes' sight, hands holding—

broken to echoes, *these
senses recreate*
their definition. I hear
the mind close.

There is
as we go we
see there
is a hairy
hole there is
a darkness ex-
panded by
there is a
sense of some
imminence imman-
ence there is
a subject placed
by the verb a
conjunction coord-
inate lines
a graph of indeterminate
feelings there is
sorry for itself
lonely generally
unhappy in its
circumstances.

THE MEASURE

I cannot
move backward
or forward.
I am caught

in the time
as measure.
What we think
of we think of—

of no other reason
we think than
just to think—
each for himself.

THE WOMAN

I have never
clearly given to you
the associations
you have for me, you

with such
divided presence my dream
does not show
you. I do not dream.

I have compounded
these sensations, the
accumulation of the things
left me by you.

Always your
tits, not breasts, but
harsh sudden rises
of impatient flesh

on the chest—is it
mine—which flower
against the vagueness
of the air you move in.

You walk
such a shortness
of intent strides, your
height is so low,

in my hand
I feel the weight
of yours there,
one over one

or both, as you
pivot upon me, the
same weight grown
as the hair, the

second of your attributes,
falls to
cover us. We
couple but lie against

no surface, have
lifted as you again
grow small
against myself, into

the air. The
air the third of
the signs you
are known by: a

quiet, a
soughing silence,
the winds lightly
moved. Then

your
mouth, it
opens not
speaking, touches,

wet, on me. Then
I scream, I
sing such as is
given to me, roar-

ing unheard,
like stark sight
sees itself
inverted

into dark
turned. Onanistic,
I feel around
myself what

you have left me
with, wetness, pools
of it, my skin
drips.

THE PATTERN

As soon as
I speak, I
speaks. It

wants to
be free but
impassive lies

in the direction
of its
words. Let

x equal x, x
also
equals x. I

speak to
hear myself
speak? I

had not thought
that some-
thing had such

undone. It
was an idea
of mine.

THE MECHANIC

Were we now to fall
to our stubborn knees
and sink to rest, my-
self sunk in yours, then

what would hold us
together but uninteresting
weight. Do you believe
love, and how much.

WALLS

Walls are
relief in lifting
themselves. Let

you also
lift yourself,
selves, shelves.

I keep to myself such
measures as I care for,
daily the rocks
accumulate position.

There is nothing
but what thinking makes
it less tangible. The mind,
fast as it goes, loses

pace, puts in place of it
like rocks simple markers,
for a way only to
hopefully come back to

where it cannot. All
forgets. My mind sinks.
I hold in both hands such weight
it is my only description.

THE DREAM

Such perfection
of dream would
first hurt, would

tear impression
from impression
making a fabric

of pain. Then
begin again
its own insistence.

In the dream
I see
two faces turned,

one of which
I assume mine, one
of which I assume.

It is
what I now make
up of it, I cannot see

more than hair
at first, a long
flowing hair there

fits it, faces
toward me as I
in it turn. Then

again pain,
for some reason, why
does it hurt. But

my feeling is,
this is what
you enjoy, so

twist to it while
the eye
of the other

face watches
me in pain. I
do not want what

I want. I dream it
in these two
painful things.

2
Why should she not
be attacked
literally. So

I attack my
mother, break
what I can reach,

the hair,
the thing I
came from.

3
If all women are
mothers, what
are men

standing
in dreams, mine
or theirs,

empty of
all but themselves.
They are so

lonely, unknown
there, I run
for whatever

is not
them, turning
into that consequence

makes me
my mother hating
myself.

4
In the day the
instruction is merely,
stand up. An

old joke relating
to the male
genital—up, up.

At night it
is the complex
as all things

are themselves and
their necessity,
even sexual. So

cunts and cocks
as eyes, noses, mouths,
have their objects:

hermaphrodite, one
sexed, bi-
sected in that lust.

5
What was the dream?
I have forgotten it
if I ever knew it

or dreamed
it more
than thinking. It

was to have been,
it was,
such I thought,

thinking. What
to dream, and what,
and what, to dream.

There was hair,
it hurt, I felt
the pain. I felt I did

I will not
change into any-
thing you don't

like if
you will stay
with me as you said

you would. Don't
go. Away.
If this is where we are.

ONE WAY

Of the two, one
faces one. In
the air there is

no tremor, no
odor. There is
a house around them,

of wood, of walls.
The mark is silence.
Everything hangs.

As he raises
his hand to
not strike her, as

again his hand
is raised, she has
gone, into another

room. In the room
left by her, he
cannot see himself

as in a mirror, as
a feeling of reflection.
He thinks he thinks,

of something else.
All the locked time,
all the letting go

down into it, as a
locked room, come to.
This time not changed,

but the way of feeling
secured by walls and books,
a picture hanging down,

a center shifted, dust
on all he puts his hand on,
disorder, papers and letters

and accumulations of clothing,
and bedclothes, and under his
feet the rug bunches.

I
The time is.
The air seems a cover,
the room is quiet.

She moves, she
had moved. He
heard her.

The children
sleep, the dog fed,
the house around them

is open, descriptive,
a truck through the walls,
lights bright there,

glaring, the sudden
roar of its motor, all
familiar impact

as it passed
so close. He
hated it.

But what does she answer.
She moves
away from it.

In all they save,
in the way of his saving
the clutter, the accumulation

of the expected disorder—
as if each dirtiness,
each blot, blurred

happily, gave
purpose, happily—
she is not enough there.

He is angry. His
face grows—as if
a moon rose

of black light,
convulsively darkening,
as if life were black.

It is black.
It is an open
hole of horror, of

nothing as if not
enough there is
nothing. A pit—

which he recognizes,
familiar, sees
the use in, a hole

for anger and
fills it
with himself,

yet watches on
the edge of it,
as if she were

not to be pulled in,
a hand could
stop him. Then

as the shouting
grows and grows
louder and louder

with spaces
of the same open
silence, the darkness,

in and out, him-
self between them,
stands empty and

holding out his
hands to both,
now screaming

it cannot be
the same, she
waits in the one

while the other
moans in the hole
in the floor, in the wall.

2

Is there some odor
which is anger,

a face
which is rage.

I think I think
but find myself in it.

The pattern
is only resemblance.

I cannot see myself
but as what I see, an

object but a man,
with lust for forgiveness,

raging, from that vantage,
secure in the purpose,

double, split.
Is it merely intention,

a sign quickly adapted,
shifted to make

a horrible place
for self-satisfaction.

I rage.
I rage, I rage.

3
You did it,
and didn't want to,

and it was simple.
You were not involved,

even if your head was cut off,
or each finger

twisted
from its shape until it broke,

and you screamed too,
with the other, in pleasure.

4
Face me,
in the dark,
my face. See me.

It is the cry
I hear all
my life, my own

voice, my
eye locked in
self sight, not

the world what
ever it is
but the close

breathing beside
me I reach out
for, feel as

warmth in
my hands then
returned. The rage

is what I
want, what
I cannot give

to myself, of
myself, in
the world.

5
After, what
is it—as if
the sun had

been wrong to return,
again. It was
another life, a

day, some
time gone, it
was done.

But also
the pleasure, the
opening

relief
even in what
was so hated.

6
All you say you want
to do to yourself you do
to someone else as yourself

and we sit between you
waiting for whatever will
be at last the real end of you.

SOME AFTERNOON

Why not ride
with pleasure
and take oneself
as measure,

making the world
tacit description
of what's taken
from it

for no good reason,
the fact only.
There is a world
elsewhere, but here

the tangible faces
smile, breaking
into tangible pieces.
I see

myself and family,
and friends, and
animals attached,
the house, the road,

all go forward
in a huge
flash, shaken
with that act.

Goodbye, goodbye.
Nothing left
after the initial
blast but

some echo like this.
Only the faded
pieces of paper
etc.

DISTANCE

I

Hadn't I been
aching, for you,
seeing the

light there, such
shape as
it makes.

The bodies
fall, have
fallen, open.

Isn't it such
a form one
wants, the warmth

as sun
light on you.
But what

were you, where,
one thought, I
was always

thinking. The
mind itself,
impulse, of form

last realized,
nothing
otherwise but

a stumbling
looking after, a
picture

of light through
dust on
an indeterminate distance,

which throws
a radiator into
edges, shining,

the woman's long
length, the move-
ment of the

child, on her,
their legs
from behind.

2
Eyes,
days and
forms' photograph,

glazed
eyes, dear
hands. We

are walking,
I have
a face grown

hairy
and old, it
has greyed

to white
on the sides
of my cheeks. Stepping

out of
the car with these
endless people,

where are
you, am I happy,
is this car

mine. Another
life comes to
its presence,

here, you
sluffing, beside
me, me off, my-

self's warmth
gone inward,
a stepping

car, walking
waters on, such
a place like the

size of great
breasts, warmth and
moisture, come

forward, waking
to that edge
of the silence.

3
The falling back
from as in
love, or

casual friend-
ship, "I am so
happy, to

meet you—" These
meetings, it is
meet

we right (write)
to one another,
the slip-

shod, half-
felt, heart's
uneasiness in

particular
forms, waking to
a body felt

as a hand pushed
between the long
legs. Is this

only the form,
"Your face
is unknown to me

but the hair, the
springing hair there
despite the rift,

the cleft,
between us, is
known, my own—"

What have they
done to me, who
are they coming

to me on such
informed feet, with
such substance of forms,

pushing
the flesh aside,
step in-

to my own,
my longing
for them.

I resolved it, I
found in my life a
center and secured it.

It is the house,
trees beyond, a term
of view encasing it.

The weather
reaches only as some
wind, a little

deadened sighing. And
if the life weren't?
when was something to

happen, had I secured
that—had I, *had*
I, insistent.

There is nothing I am,
nothing not. A place
between, I am. I am

more than thought, less
than thought. A house
with winds, but a distance

—something loose in the wind,
feeling weather as that life,
walks toward the lights he left.

SONG

I wouldn't
embarrass you
ever.

If there were
not place
or time for it,

I would go,
go elsewhere,
remembering.

I would
sit in a
flower, a face, not

to embarrass
you, would
be unhappy

quietly, would
never
make a noise.

Simpler,
simpler you
deal with me.

What do you
want, love. To be
loved. What,

what wanted,
love, wanted
so much as love

like nothing
considered, no
feeling but

a simple
recognition
forgotten sits

in its feeling,
two things,
one and one.

FOR HELEN

       . . . If I can
remember anything, it
is the way ahead
you made for me, specifically:

    wet-
ness, now the grass
as early it
has webs, all the lawn
stretched out from
the door, the back
one with a small crabbed
porch. The trees
are, then, so high,
a huge encrusted
sense of grooved trunk,
I can
slide my finger along
each edge.

A NIGHT SKY

All the grass
dies
in front of us.

The fire
again
flares out.

The night
such a large
place. Stars

the points
but like
places no

depth, I see
a flat—
a plain as if the

desert
were showing smaller
places.

THE ANSWER

Will we speak to each other
making the grass bend as if
a wind were before us, will our

way be as graceful, as
substantial as the movement
of something moving so gently.

We break things in pieces like
walls we break ourselves into
hearing them fall just to hear it.

DIMENSIONS

1
Little places as
size of
one hand, shrink

to one finger
as tall
as, I am

sitting
down even
smaller.

2
Think if
understanding is
what you
had thought

of it, in
it you think
a picture
comes and

goes, re-
flected there
large faces
float but

no harm comes
to the sleeping
princess
ever.

3
My voice is
a foot. My
head is

a foot. I
club
people in

my mind, I
push them this
way, that

way, from
the little
way

I see them
up
the length,

for fear
of being hurt
they fall.

A PLACE

The wetness of that street, the light,
the way the clouds were heavy is
not description. But in the memory I fear

the distortion. I do not feel
what it was I was feeling. I am impatient to begin again, open

whatever door it was, find the weather
is out there, grey, the rain then and
now falling from the sky to the wet ground.

SOME ECHOES

Some echoes,
little pieces,
falling, a dust,

sunlight, by
the window, in
the eyes. Your

hair as
you brush
it, the light

behind
the eyes,
what is left of it.

FANCY

Do you know what
the truth is,
what's rightly
or wrongly said,

what is wiseness,
or rightness, what
wrong, or well-
done if it is,

or is not, done.
I thought.
I thought and
thought and thought.

In a place
I was sitting,
and there
it was, a little

faint thing
hardly felt, a
kind of small
nothing.

THE WORLD

I wanted so ably
to reassure you, I wanted
the man you took to be me,

to comfort you, and got
up, and went to the window
pushed back, as you asked me to,

the curtain, to see
the outline of the trees
in the night outside.

The light, love,
the light we felt then,
greyly, was it, that

came in, on us, not
merely my hands or yours,
or a wetness so comfortable,

but in the dark then
as you slept, the grey
figure came so close

and leaned over,
between us, as you
slept, restless, and

my own face had to
see it, and be seen by it,
the man it was, your

grey lost tired bewildered
brother, unused, untaken—
hated by love, and dead,

but not dead, for an
instant, saw me, myself
the intruder, as he was not.

I tried to say, it is
all right, she is
happy, you are no longer

needed. I said,
he is dead, and he
went as you shifted

and woke, at first afraid,
then knew by my own knowing
what had happened—

and the light then
of the sun coming
for another morning
in the world.

GOING

There is nothing
to turn from,
or to, no

way other
than forward, such
place as I mark

time. Let me
leave here a
mark, a

way through
her mind.

Not from that
could you get it,
nor can things
comprise a form

just to be made.
Again, let
each be this or
that, they, together,

are many whereas,
one by one,
each is a wooden
or metal or even

water, or vegetable,
flower, a crazy orange
sun, a windy
dirt, and here is

a place to sit
shaded by tall buildings
and a bed that
grows leaves on

all its branches
which are
boards I know
soon enough.

WORDS

You are always
with me,
there is never
a separate

place. But if
in the twisted
place I
cannot speak,

not indulgence
or fear only,
but a tongue
rotten with what

it tastes—There is
a memory
of water, of
food, when hungry.

Some day
will not be
this one, then
to say

words like a
clear, fine
ash sifts,
like dust,

from nowhere.

Each gesture
is a common one, a
black dog, crying, a
man, crying.

All alike, people
or things grow
fixed with what
happens to them.

I throw a stone.
It hits the wall,
it hits a dog,
it hits a child—

my sentimental
names for years
and years ago, from
something I've not become.

If I look
in the mirror,
the wall, I
see myself.

If I try
to do better
and better, I
do the same thing.

Let me hit you.
Will it hurt.
Your face is hurt
all the same.

THE SHAME

What will
the shame be,
what
cost to pay.

We are walking
in a wood,
wood of stones,
boulders for trees.

The sky
is a black
sudden cloud,
a sun.

Speak
to me, say
what things
were forgotten.

THE STATUE

I propose to you
a body bleached, a body
which would be dead
were it not alive.

We will stand it up
in the garden which
we have taken such pains
to water. All the flowers

will grow at its feet
and evenings it will
soften there as the darkness
comes down from such space.

Perhaps small sounds
will come from it, perhaps
the wind only, but its
mouth, could one see it,

will flutter. There will be
a day it walks just before
we come to look at it, but by then
it will have returned to its place.

THE WINDOW

There will be no simple
way to avoid what
confronts me. Again and
again I know it, but

take heart, hopefully,
in the world unavoidably
present. Here, I think,
is a day, not a
but the. My hands are

shaking, there is
an insistent tremble
from the night's
drinking. But what

was I after, you
were surely open to me.
Out the far window
there was such intensity

of yellow light. But love,
love I so wanted I
got, didn't I, and then
fell senseless, with relief.

TO BOBBIE

What can occur
invests the weather, also,
but the trees, again,
are in bloom.

The day will not
be less than that. I
am writing to you,
wishing to be rid of

these confusions. You
have so largely
let me continue, not
as indulgence but

then to say I
have said, and will,
anything is so
hard, at this moment.

In my mind, as
ever, you occur. Your
face is such
delight, I can

see the lines there
as the finest
mark of ourselves.
Your skin at moments

is translucent. I
want to make love
to you, now. The world
is the trees, you,

I cannot change it,
the weather
occurs, the mind
is not its only witness.